Goodbye Poverty

&

Hello
Abundance

CORINA MAUSALI

Author of "Your Will Be Done, 30 Day Devotions"

Published in the United States by Sent One Publishing, Seattle, WA 98178

Goodbye Poverty & Hello Abundance

Unless otherwise noted, all Scriptures are taken from the Holy Bible. Scripture references marked NKJV are taken from the New King James Version, © 1979, 1980, 1982 by Thomas Nelson, Inc. Used by permission.

Scripture references marked NIV are taken from the New International Version, © 2004-2007 by Bible Hub. Used by permission.

Scripture references marked NLT are taken from the New Living Translation, © 2004-2007 by Bible Hub. Used by permission.

Scripture references marked AMP are taken from the Amplified Version, © 1995-2017. Used by permission of Zondervan. All rights reserved worldwide.

Scripture references marked MSG are taken from the Message Version, © 1995-2017. Used by permission of Zondervan. All rights reserved worldwide.

ISBN-13: 978-0692-08461-8
ISBN-10: 0692084614

Dedication

This book is dedicated to those who are tired of having the same money issues and not getting any *new results*. I was tired of having those same issues, so now I am enjoying a piece of my *new results*.

Table of Contents

Thank You Page

First and foremost, I would like to thank God and give Him all the glory, honor, and praise for everything He has done, will do, and is doing in my life.

I thank my parents Junior and Fiaaliali Mausali, for bringing me into this world and raising me the best way possible.

I give thanks to my husband Eric Payne who has been by my side in this journey, bearing with me for the countless nights of the lights being on just so I could finish my writing.

I also want to thank my children, Unity and Uriah, for being a blessing to me, and for being my motivation to keep pressing in.

To the rest of my family including my in-laws, thank you for being who you all are, and for motivating me to improve myself by strongly moving forward on my journey.

I'd like to thank my church family, InPursuit Ministry, for being there for me and my family, and for always loving us with open arms like a true church.

Thank you to my Apostle Deborah Vails and Set Free Outreach Ministry family, who continues to teach me to walk in my purpose and calling.

Thank you to my Writing Coach/Minister, Catherine Storing, who has been challenging me since the summer to get this book out, and for all the nuggets she shared in her books, not to mention introducing me to SAX WORSHIP MUSIC which has helped me get through my days of writing.

Thank you to my Writing Made Simple Family. Thank you for being there with me up to the finish line.

Special thanks to my dear friend, Rovila De Guzman, who has been my cheerleader through this whole project. You rock, friend! Thank you for the listening ear and the positive feedbacks.

I want to thank my anointed book designer, Elisha Scott of Elisha Scott Studio, who is also a scribe and very talented at bringing things to life with her creations. You are such a blessing to me.

Last but not the least; I want to thank Prophetess Maria-Elisa Maki, my editor, another scribe who God led me to during this project. I am so grateful for you as well and I thank God for our divine connection and your many words of encouragement!

Introduction

So many people are walking around with this gray cloud over their heads, which they cannot seem to get away from. It is the storm of a "broke" mentality, a mindset that has been passed down from one generation to the next. It is a distorted belief system about wealth, the kind of poverty mindset that keeps us broke, because we think that money is the only way we can be rich.

I will share with you, in this book, the things I have been through that kept me bound. I will also share with you steps I took to get out of this poverty mindset and what I'm doing to maintain what I have accomplished, while I continue to grow and level up in life.

I too came from a place of brokenness. I know what it's like living on a budget. I have experienced losing everything in one night, and then seeing God swoop in and restore what was gone. I have struggled being a single mom trying to make it in this world but not letting anything stop me.

I wrote this book for those who are tired of being in a financial strain and looking for the sun through the gray clouds. My own tiredness being in the dark about wealth made me write my way through those clouds.

This book will make you learn about some mistakes I have made, which will help you avoid making the same. Likewise, you will learn what you can do to break free from your old mindsets and create a healthy, wealthy life you have always hoped for.

As you can see, this is proof of me saying, "Goodbye to Poverty and Hello to Abundance." I am not saying that you too should write a book, but if it's in you, by all means go for it. This is just part of the step to walking into the fullness of what God has in store for me like He has for you.

Don't delay and let others pass you up in getting to that place of wealth because they snatched up this book. So, let's get you on track by breaking up with that poverty mindset RIGHT NOW!

Find out what my biggest money leak was and what kept me getting up, learning, and showing up. Discover how I changed my mind to the things I was willing to surrender to God, and to what I am planting for a latter harvest, while waiting for the abundance to rain on me.

Section One
Identifying My Money Story

Entry 1

I don't think it ever crossed my mind that my family lacked money. My Dad always provided for our family, so we never went without; or at least from what I saw. There were eight of us in my family, my parents and us six girls. The minute my three younger sisters were old enough to go to school, my Mom went back out into the workforce to help my Dad with earning income for the family. As I think back a little harder, I remember a time when I was about nine and whenever we would go to the store, whether it was to the grocery or department store, I wouldn't pick out much or choose anything expensive even though my Mom did allow me to get something. I would pick something inexpensive or cheap because there were too many of us and I didn't want my Mom to spend money on something I really didn't need. I guess that's when I realized it but was not aware of it until now, that money was scarce in my family. After asking myself the question again, "When did I learn money was scarce in my family?" flash backs of memories started coming up to mind. But first, I had to make sure I understood the meaning of the word "scarce." My definition of the word is not having much. For those who don't know, Merriam-Webster's definition is: deficient in quantity or number compared with the demand; not plentiful or abundant. Basically, it's having lack of or too little of.

Now back to that memory. I remember we were living in Seattle until after I completed preschool, and then we moved to California because of my Dad's job. My Dad was a very smart man and wanted the best for his family, like our Heavenly Father wants for us. As kids back then, we had all we wanted, and even more. But then, when I was seven, something happened that we decided to move back to Seattle. Prior to any of us kids being born, my Dad bought two homes in Seattle. He purchased one for his Grandmother, who raised him and his little sister. The other house he gave to my Grandparents on my Mom's side. Somehow, the family ended up losing both houses. So, when we moved back to Seattle from California, we had to start all over again.

Our family moved into the projects known as High Point and we stayed there for about four and a half years. During this time, we were utilizing the resources out there to help us, like receiving government assistance and going to food and clothing banks. Then, God gave my Dad the strength and wisdom to do it again. He took us out of the projects and bought our family another house in the Skyway area, where I currently live. As my sisters and I were old enough to legally work, we took on part-time jobs and summer jobs to help out with the bills. Of course, my Mom would give my sisters and I an allowance from what we made, which I didn't mind most of the time. I was just happy to pitch in and also get a little bit of cash while I was at it. Honestly, despite the move from California to Seattle and living in the projects, I never thought we had a problem with money. It looked as if everything was under control. I didn't know that there were more things going on that were not obvious to me, things that I thought were just normal, not realizing what it really meant. These things that looked normal included not leaving the water running while washing dishes, turning the lights off when we leave the room, mom working double shifts, and dad working overtime – all these to save bills and live in a house we own. Society did paint a picture that if you own your home with a picket fence and have two cars, you have made it.

Having my own family, I know now what my parents were going through and why they pushed us hard to stay in school and do well. They wanted us to avoid the same hardship they've experienced. This is something all parents who love their children do, to the best of their abilities.

I had my own share of being on government assistance, standing in food bank lines, and signing up for the programs the community would have during holidays. There were many things I have done in my past that I am not proud of, but it was all a learning lesson which has brought me where I am today.

When did you first learn that your family had lack of or did not have enough of money?

_____

_____

_____

_____

_____

What are some of the things you do financially that stems from what you've learned?

_____

_____

_____

_____

_____

_____

_____

Now that you are aware of these things, it is time to do something about it.

Entry 2

Broke has kept me small so many times in the past. Some of the lies it would tell me would try to keep me from getting what I should receive. I never really thought about money like most people do. I know it's part of a necessity in life, and I know people need money to survive and provide for themselves and their families. One of the lies "broke" told me was, it's okay to live beneath my means. It's okay to stay on the welfare system because I get free money and food stamps that wouldn't even last me a month. It's okay to live on Section 8 and never own my own home. Why would I want to pay for a mortgage when I can pay only 30% of my income to live in a home they approve of? Oh, you want to start a business? Here comes another broke lie. Well, you need to have a certain amount of money to start a business and you need to have a business degree. I even had thoughts about not being able to publish my first book because I was looking at how much it was going to cost me and the lies were saying it's way too much. This is a cycle of cheapness that has plagued me; but God intervened and showed me what I needed to do.

Actually, I have been searching for a home to purchase for over a year and a half now, and sometimes the prices would make me think otherwise because "broke" said I can't afford it. But I believe God wants me to have the desires of my heart. If my desires are lined up with His, He will make it happen because He is who He says He is and that's that.

Broke almost kept me from taking a promotion earlier this year with the company I am currently employed at. But God's Word came to the rescue.

2 Timothy 1:7(KJV)
For God hath not given us the spirit of fear, but of power, and of love, and of a sound mind.

Jeremiah 29:11(NIV)

"For I know the plans I have for you," declares the Lord, "plans to prosper you and not harm you, plans to give you hope and a future."

It was a struggle at first but God brought me through it all and continues to. His Word says in Matthew 7:7-8 (NIV) "Ask and it will be given to you; seek and you will find; knock and the door will be opened to you. For everyone who asks receives; the one who seeks finds; and the one who knocks, the door will be opened." He answered my prayers and continues to answer the prayers of others by me accepting that promotion.

Being broke or having that kind of mindset is crippling, and if I had continued with that type of mindset I probably would not have done half of the things I have done since the Summer of 2016 up until this moment.

I see so many people who allow "broke" be the reason they cannot do anything and I see what it does when they speak it over themselves. If they only knew the power in their words, they probably would change the way they speak to others and over their own lives. I had to learn that myself and still have to be reminded sometimes. Yes, we quote the scripture Proverbs 18:21 (AMP) "Death and life are in the power of the tongue, and those who love it and indulge it will eat its fruit and bear the consequences of their words." But how many of us actually believe it? It took me a minute to get that to sink in. We also read in Psalm 33:9 "For He spoke, and it was done; He commanded, and it stood fast." So, if we are the children of the Most High and understand that God has given us all the power and authority, why are we still in this broke place? He tells us in John 14:12 that whoever believes in Him will not only do the works that He did but greater. We have the power to speak life into things and not death. In Proverbs 23:7 (AMP) "For as he thinks in his heart, so is he." So when we think we are "broke" and say we are, then that is exactly what we become and we eat the fruit thereof. From this day forward, I am giving "broke" its eviction papers. You no longer reside here and whatever little hiding spot you thought you had here, is officially closed and boarded up. Adios!

How many times has "broke" kept you down?

_____

What are ALL the lies that "broke" have been telling you?

_____

_____

_____

_____

_____

Enough is enough! It's time for you to make a declaration right here and right now. Make sure when you read the declaration to read it out loud so your inner self can hear it. With authority, say it and mean it, if you are truly tired of living broke and beneath your means.

Declaration:

I am done being broke. NO MORE!!! The cycle of being broke ends with me. The cycle of poverty ends with me and ends right now. The cycle of lies and excuses ends with me and ends right now. I will not take this with me on my next journey or level. Adios broke! Ciao! Hasta la vista! I am slamming and locking the doors and closing all windows to you! So long and never to return!

You can also make a list of everything you are not comfortable with and fill in the blanks to add to your own personal declaration. Say it as many times to yourself and make it even more personal by looking in the mirror and saying it. I know it may sound dumb but if we let "broke" talk us out of our blessings we can surely talk ourselves into it.

Example:

The cycle of _____ ends with me and ends
right now.

Entry 3

I am not happy living in the small two-bedroom duplex we are currently living in. I am grateful and blessed to have a roof over our heads but I cannot take living here anymore. I want a bigger place we can call our very own and being able to leave it behind to our children and grandchildren when we leave this earth. I deal with leaving and coming to this small box every day with a feeling of anger in some way. I want out! This place is not for me and if I stay it will kill who I am supposed to be and created to be. I feel restrained living in this place. I feel cramped and almost like it's choking the air out of me. I am not free to move around like I really want to or use some of the things we have stored up in the attic because there is no room to keep it at arm's reach. I find myself spending money on items I probably have stored in the attic because it will be a hassle for my husband to go digging through the boxes to find it. I am not saying that he wouldn't, but on his time. I like to have an actual living room where I can enjoy the company of my family and friends. As I said before, it is

21

a two-bedroom but we turned the small living room into another bedroom, which we sleep in. My youngest daughter occupies one of the bedrooms and the other official bedroom, we use as a guest room for anyone that stays a night. I also use the other bedroom to read, write and spend time with God when no one is occupying it. I would like to have my own little office where I can do all my writing, reading, and spending time with God without any interruptions or feeling like I have to go somewhere else because someone is sleeping in there. I don't like the area we live in either due to the many hills we have to climb or go down. When it snows, we cannot get out without meeting up with a hill. Everywhere we go and turn there are hills. I don't mind looking at hills God created but those hills are not for me, especially in the snow. Those hills are for the birds, the stray cats and dogs in the neighborhood and for anyone else that don't mind living there. Yes, we live in a small box called a duplex but I have not made it my home. I know it's just a "pit stop" for me as that is how I feel about living here. I have made up my mind and have decided that 2017 is it. I will finish out this year living here and next year for sure we will be moving into our new place we can call our very own. No more letters of rent increase or having to walk outside to get to the laundry room. No more many hills to climb or waiting on a maintenance guy to do repairs. I declare and decree that no lease or amount will stop us from moving into our new home in 2018 in Jesus' mighty name. My God is my provider. He is Jehovah Jireh. He will make a way like I know and trust He will because He always does. My God! Thank You Lord!!!

Isaiah 43:16-19 (NKJV)
Thus says the Lord, who makes a way in the sea
And a path through the mighty waters,
[17] Who brings forth the chariot and horse,
The army and the power
(They shall lie down together, they shall not rise;
They are extinguished, they are quenched like a wick):
[18] "Do not remember the former things,

Nor consider the things of old.

¹⁹ Behold, I will do a new thing,

Now it shall spring forth;

Shall you not know it?

I will even make a road in the wilderness

And rivers in the desert."

By us moving into a bigger place and purchasing our own home, we will be investing in ourselves and our children. We can freely move around and do all things without feeling restrained or limited. We will probably have a little more bills than we have now but it is nothing we cannot handle. As a married couple, we will have met one of our goals and are ready to accomplish even more. This is just a piece of what God is doing and wants to do in our lives.

Write down what it would look like if you make up your mind to want more.

_____

_____

_____

_____

What is it that you are choosing to say No to and whatever or whomever it is that is NOT lining up with the EXTRAODINARY AWESOME person God created you to be?

_____

_____

_____

_____

_____

_____

Entry 4

As I sit here thinking about what kind of phrases or thoughts I have been using to hide behind, I came up with nothing. My mind drew a blank. I tried to think harder: "savings – trying to save" and "waiting for the right or perfect time." After listening to Catherine Storing's devotions, the phrase "I've been doing it by myself" stood out strong for me. I don't know about anyone else but it had my name all over it.

Being a wife, I would discuss things with my husband regarding anything I would consider as a big decision to make. One of those big decisions would be purchasing a home or taking trips. So, going back to the phrases or thoughts that I came up with at the beginning of my entry, those seem more like my husbands' phrases or thoughts. He is always talking about us needing to save more money and save as much money as we can before we can make any big purchases. He is also waiting for the right and perfect time. But what if the right and perfect time is now? If I brought this before my husband, he would say, "that's what if, but we need to think realistically." Of course, I would get upset because "what if" we miss the "perfect and right time?"

Many dedicated hardworking people will work all their lives to save up and never really get the opportunity to enjoy the fruits of their labor and some may even die before that ever happens. I refuse to be one of them. I am not saying that people shouldn't save. But sometimes we have to do something different to get a different result and sometimes that requires taking a risk. Wouldn't you want to take a risk and know that at least you tried and if it didn't work, it's okay you can just start again? I would rather try and fail than to not try at all and then forever have it in the back of my mind, "what if" or "if only I did this." We have to step out of the mundane routine. We have to step out in faith like I'm doing with this book. I don't know who's going to read this and like it but that's a risk I am willing to take. Life is about taking risks. Every choices and decisions we make is a risk to the paths we take because there are consequences we will have to face in the end. Some may be good results and some may be bad, but it's never too bad that we can't turn around and do it right the next time.

When I don't get the kind of support I feel I should get, I go into my independent mode. The "I'm going to do this by myself" attitude comes out. If I wait on my husband, I might as well just forget about moving or going anywhere. Messing with him, we are never moving to our own home or taking a trip he will plan. So, what does Corina do? She will do what she does best. She will start doing her research. Of course, I am doing this all by myself. This is the famous phrase and thought I tend to hide behind. Why do I need to do that when I should approach it from a different angle? Let's take our simple trip to Las Vegas as an example. I started looking for local places for us to visit because I was still waiting on my husband to plan our trip. I can go on and on about my husband taking his time but I need to be creative in my thinking and suggestions.

Maybe I can help my husband by doing the research for our trip and let him make the final decisions on all the information I have gathered. It will be like it was his decision in the end. Then I won't be doing this by myself. The important thing is, I need to remember to seek God in all that I do. It is He who will order my steps in the way I should go. He is the light unto my path. I may want to take a trip right now and the Lord will send an angel to deter me from taking that trip because there is something else God may need for me to do or somewhere He may need me to be. We never know what is going on in the other realm but when we are in tune with the Lord, we become more aware of it and have a better understanding why things are moving and happening the way they are. Therefore, no matter what I do or face, reading and meditating on the scriptures will help me and can help you as well get through the times of uncertainty.

1 Chronicles 16:11 (AMP)
Seek the Lord and His strength;

Seek His face continually [longing to be in His presence].

Judges 6:16 (AMP)

The Lord answered him, "I will certainly be with you, and you will strike down the Midianites as [if they were only] one man."

Deuteronomy 31:6 (NKJV)

"Be strong and of good courage, do not fear nor be afraid of them; for the Lord your God, He is the One who goes with you. He will not leave you nor forsake you."

1 Corinthians 10:13 (NKJV)

No temptation has overtaken you except such as is common to man; but God is faithful, who will not allow you to be tempted beyond what you are able, but with the temptation will also make the way of escape, that you may be able to bear it.

What phrases or thoughts are you hiding behind?

_____

_____

_____

_____

Whatever it is, it has to go. Time to clean house!
Now you can choose your thoughts and feelings that
you want to have throughout your day every day.
When a thought comes to mind that does not equal to
what God says about you then rebuke it with His Word.

Psalm 139:14 (AMP)
I will give thanks and praise to You, for I am fearfully
and wonderfully made;
Wonderful are Your works,
And my soul knows it very well.

Entry 5

I am no longer listening to the lies the enemy has so enjoyed telling me for all these years and about what I have coming on account of my relationship with our Father, the Creator of the Universe. I am replacing the lies of telling me it's okay to stay mediocre because that's where I need to be or was created to be. I am replacing the lies that I am not going to be successful like the other Authors and that nobody wants to read my books. I am replacing the lies of what people are saying and speaking towards me because I don't fit what they call qualified, to do the work God set out for me to do. God qualifies anyone who He chooses NOT who man (hu-MAN) chooses. He will take the foolish to confound the wise. My God says, whatever I ask in His Name, I shall receive and He will give me the desires of my heart. God told me to write this book like He told me to write the first book. Because this book is being written right now and will be published shortly after, this book is already a success. Whether one person reads it or more, I obeyed the voice of the Lord and this book will do exactly what God set it out to do.

I am taking the promises God has for His people and I will stand on it and I am expecting for them to come to pass.

Exodus 14:14(NIV)
The Lord will fight for you; you need only to be still.

Isaiah 41:13(NIV)
For I am the Lord your God who takes hold of your right hand and says to you, Do not fear; I will help you.

Deuteronomy 31:8(NIV)
The Lord himself goes before you and will be with you; He will never leave you nor forsake you. Do not be afraid; do not be discouraged.

Mark 11:24(NIV)

Therefore I tell you, whatever you ask for in prayer, believe that you have received it, and it will be yours.

Philippians 4:19(NIV)

And my God will meet all your needs according to the riches of His glory in Christ Jesus.

By sharing with others the knowledge that I have been given, I can create abundance for them and many others they will meet along the way. When we can continue the process of sharing the wealth of knowledge and teaching, there is so much more wealth gain than just monetary. God our Father said we will be seated at the right side of Jesus and rule and reign with Him. Hence, it is time for us to stand on that word and believe in the Power God has given to us. We need to do the work to enlarge our territories, wherever those territories God has placed us in. We need to go beyond the boundaries of the church circle and reach out to those outside by bringing the Kingdom of God to them and wherever we tread our foot upon. I will take my place in and rule whatever God has promised to give me for my promised land. Some of us will have to take it by force spiritually. I know I will NO longer sit back and let the enemy steal my blessings or the blessings of my family and children. NO MORE!!! Thank You Father for the strategies you will give me on how to go about this and how to take over the land you are sending me to, in Jesus' mighty name, Amen.

You can replace the lies the enemy has been telling you about what you deserve or should receive on behalf of your relationship with our Heavenly Father with some of those promises I have mentioned.

Now that you know a few promises the Creator has for us, how does that make you feel reading it and making it personal?

_____

_____

_____

_____

There are many more promises in the Bible that I have not listed, and if it really has helped you along your journey write it below; or write a new one that is speaking to you for this new journey you are treading on.

_____

_____

_____

_____

You can always come back to remind yourself the promises God has spoken. He is a promise keeper not a promise breaker!

Entry 6

I believe I have wasted so much time not doing what
God has called me to do. All those years of not
knowing the truth had me living beneath my calling and
gifts. I had accepted living spiritually illegal on this earth
for over 40 years. I feel like I was Moses and the people
of Israel being in the wilderness for 40 years when it
should have only taken them 11 days. Why? Because I
wanted to do things my own way and not God's. I was
fearful and disobedient. The Creator has a plan for all of
us and the Holy Bible is Life's Instruction Manual on
how to live on this earth.

Ephesians 4:21-25 (MSG) "But that's no life for you.
You learned Christ! My assumption is that you have
paid careful attention to Him, been well instructed in
the truth precisely as we have it in Jesus. Since, then, we
do not have the excuse of ignorance, everything – and I
do mean everything – connected with that old way of
life has to go. It's rotten through and through. Get rid

of it! And then take on an entirely new way of life – a God fashioned life, a life renewed from the inside and working itself into your conduct as God accurately reproduces His character in you. What this adds up to, then, is this: no more lies, no more pretense. Tell your neighbor the truth. In Christ's body we're all connected to each other, after all. When you lie to others, you end up lying to yourself."

God opened my eyes to His Truth. Like in Isaiah 35:5 "Then the eyes of the blind will be opened and the ears of the deaf will be opened." The more I get into His Word and spend time with Him, the more I learn about His Kingdom and myself. The Bible says in John 10:10(KJV) "…I am come that they might have life, and that they might have it more abundantly." If I say, I am a child of the Most High God and He says, I am an heir in His Kingdom, then why am I living beneath the means God has promised me? For He has given me all the power and authority over every living creature and that I have been given the instructions to multiply and be fruitful with all He has given me.

I have been improperly using my gifts over 40 years for the world and self-gain and not for the Kingdom of God. I didn't think the things I am good at really mattered or counted to anyone. I didn't think it was something I could offer to anyone or to the Kingdom of God and that I would prosper from it. I just thought they were hobbies and nobody really has any need for it. But I know now that was and is a lie from the enemy to keep me from becoming who God has created me to be and needs me to be. I choose today, to no longer live illegal in any seasons of my life. I choose to live spiritually legal in the Kingdom of God and knowing who I am and whose I am. I choose to live life more abundantly and will use my gifts for the Kingdom to share the goodness of God and what He has done in my life and continues to do. According to Luke 4:18 "The Spirit of the Lord is upon me, because He anointed me to preach the gospel to the poor. He has sent me to proclaim release to the captives, and recovery of sight to the blind, to set free those who are oppressed." It is time people of God to be set free from the poverty mindset.

John 8:36(NIV)
So, if the Son makes you free, you will be free indeed.

Let's give it all unto the Lord for His yoke is easy and His burden is light. Let go and let God do His work. If you have tried it your way and still nothing is working, it is time to do something new to get new results. Trust in the Lord with all your heart, mind, body, and soul right where you are and watch Him do it for you when you make your requests known before Him.

How many years have you been living beneath your calling and gifts? It's time we flip those negative numbers into positive ones for the new seasons we are walking into. Let's not give our time to things that are not profitable for our eternal well-being.

Section Two
Knowing & Understanding My Numbers

Entry 7

Thinking about what could be the biggest leak my family has, I would have to say shopping (grocery/herbs/misc.). Since we have changed our eating habits and diet, we are always buying groceries. It seems like almost every other day, if not two to three times out of the week.

My husband Eric and I have stopped eating meat for about a year now. We still eat seafood. Slowly but surely, we will be on our way to just eating plant-based foods. What we used to spend on meat goes to most of the produce we buy and then some on seafood. I feel like we have saved more money by eating this way and also growing some of our own vegetables as well.

Eric started doing research on herbs and plants for medicinal use and that is where the other portion of our money goes now besides our monthly bills. Also, I tend to buy things for others and helping out one of my sisters who I see strive to make ends meet for her and her daughter. Being a single mother before, I know what it's like. God blessed me with two beautiful daughters I have raised on my own financially. I know how it feels to want to take a break and actually get one or even a helping hand that is not expecting to get anything back in return. But that is why I am there to help her whether she asks for it or not. Like her, I vowed that I would do all I can to provide for my children whether their fathers were in the picture or not. I would hardly ever ask for money from anyone. I was Ms. Independent. If I had to ask for money from anyone in my family, they knew it was serious because I was not the person to ask for help. So, being the person I am and the things I have gone through, I do my best to help my sisters and others by sharing with them some of the things that worked for me, whether it was financially or not, and how to go about it.

After my divorce with my first husband, I was spending my money on shopping because I could. But was it a smart thing to do? I think not. I was more hurt that spending my money was supposedly the cure to making me feel better, but it still didn't fill that void. One thing for sure is, I wouldn't spend any money until after my bills were all taken care of. Nowadays I have to act like the "Money Police," with my husband Eric when he asks to buy more herbs, since I am the one who handles all the bills.

Currently, I am working in an Accounting Department for a tech company. I never would have imagined working in that type of position. In school I never really cared for math. It wasn't like I didn't know how to do it; I just didn't find any interest in it like I do with reading, writing, and arts. The first time I used Excel back in 2000, we didn't get along and that was just the basics. Fast forward now into 2017, I stay using Excel daily in the position I am in. I'm not saying I'm an expert, but I continue to learn new functions and formulas. It's funny how God make things work out for our good.

He answered my prayer about giving me a position with this company. One of my sisters told me, don't pray for a job; pray for a position. Immediately after she told me that, I went home and I prayed to God for a position. I went from a contract employee to a permanent employee within 11 months and then promoted to another position after a year, without ever applying for any of the positions.

1 Peter 5:6-7 (NLT)
Humble yourselves under the mighty power of God, and at the right time He will lift (promote) you up in honor. Give all your worries and cares to God, for He cares about you.

The last position I had, God made it available for me. I was working as a temp for almost about a year with this company and then they offered me a permanent position they just created for me. When we stay humble and do our assignments unto the Lord, He will open doors for us. He did it for me. He can do it for you.

Proverbs 18:6 (KJV)
A man's gift maketh room for him, and bringeth him before great men.

Honestly, it was all God who brought me to this company and also promoted me twice and gave the increase.

1 Corinthians 3:7 (KJV)
So then neither is he that planteth anything, neither he that watereth; but God that giveth the increase.

Last year, God was teaching me to put money aside for myself. I would give God His 10% first, then give myself 10% of what was left after God, then 30% on groceries/hygiene/miscellaneous items, and 50% for bills and that would be the 100% Spending Rule. If I went over the percentage in any categories, then there was something wrong in how I was spending and managing our money. I was doing it for a few months and it really came in handy when I needed it. I called it my "Rainy Day" money. This takes discipline and consistency if you really want to see your money grow. We pay everyone else but we don't pay ourselves and that was one thing I liked about it. For example, when something was wrong with my car, I had that money to help instead of touching anything that was already spoken for. I know now what I need to cut out and it's whatever or whoever that's taking from me and not pouring back into me. I know what works for me and I will have to discipline myself in being consistent to keep pushing until I break through.

I said all that to say this, we have to know our numbers before we can truly understand them.

What is your BIGGEST leak?

_____

_____

_____

_____

Now that you know, what are you going to do to
eliminate it? Write down some steps you will take to put
this into action.

_____

_____

_____

_____

_____

_____

_____

Entry 8

I have been praying for the salvation of people and for them to come to know Christ, have a personal relationship with Him, be delivered and healed, but not really thinking about praying for "more" in relation to financial wants or needs. For I know my God provides and there is nothing that He can't or will not do for His children who ask. Recently my prayers would be for God to help me find a home for my family but not being specific in details. Like a house big enough for all of my family to live in with good sewage system, no walls-cupboards-racks that look like it's being held together with bubble gum or uneven doors, floors and ceilings. Lord, let the home You will bless us with have wood floorings, with a window over the kitchen sink, windows in the bathrooms, 5 bedrooms, laundry room inside the home, 2 fireplaces, 2-car garage, and a big yard with good soil for planting, and that I am able to walk around the outside of my home with no blockage. Lord, make the entrance way to get in the house flat so it will be easy for my mom to walk in and out of and that there would be a bedroom on the main floor close to the bathroom for my mom as well. This would be part of my prayer to God for "more." I would also include on my prayer list more God-ideas, more plans and strategies on what kind of business to start, what it will all entail, and the process of how to go about it and complete it, in Jesus' name, Amen. If I were to make a list of all that I want and need, it wouldn't be that long because of what I want for now are the ones I have just listed earlier. Lord, I come before you in the mighty name of Jesus. As You have heard me in the beginning of this entry regarding the house I am praying for and making it known to you, I pray Father for Your help in finding this home in either the Tukwila or Burien area for us. We have 2 vehicles and one is not being used (Bertha-my husband's pickup) because of expired tabs and it doesn't want to start and the other one (Casper-Crossover SUV) we are running like crazy and we definitely are overdue for another vehicle. I pray my husband Eric will get things straightened out with his truck and his license. Lord, send us the help we need to accomplish the things you need for us to do. Put us before or in front of the right real estate agent, car dealership, or person. Thank You Lord for hearing my prayers and working it out right now in Jesus' mighty name, Amen.

Right now, I make about $40,000 plus a year but I would like to make more than that. I want my annual income to be what my husband and I make combined. This will give me the opportunity to help others without feeling I am being restrained and that I don't have to take from my savings to be able to give. I want to be able to move into our new home next year 2018 and still be of help to others, even when my husband gets laid off due to construction projects being completed because he works for the union. I want to start my own business and be able to help others by making opportunities available for them to work on projects that God blesses me with.

My youngest daughter has worked hard saving up her money from prior summer jobs to buy her first car. I would like to be able to help purchase one for her without any restrictions. I would rather have her invest her money into something that will financially help her in the future.

This is the reason in this season I am learning something new on how to become wealthy spiritually, mentally, and physically. This is the beginning of a new financial journey in my life which the Lord is taking me on.

Thank You Lord for the freedom to walk in liberty in You and to receive ALL that You have for me in the fullness thereof!!!

How much is the need that you have been praying for?

_____

_____

_____

_____

Write down ALL your NEEDS, and even list the amount because there is NO limit with God. When you are done, bring it before Him in prayer. Let your requests be made known.

_____

_____

_____

_____

_____

_____

Now how do you feel that you made ALL your requests known to God?

_____

_____

_____

_____

_____

God wants to hear from us. Yes, He already knows what we are going to ask before we do it but He wants to hear it from our mouths. He wants us to speak it into existence like He did when He created the world. He said, "let there be light" and so there was. Practice bringing ALL your NEEDS to Him first. The Bible tells us to "seek ye FIRST the Kingdom of God and His righteousness and everything else will be added unto you."

Hebrews 4:16 (KJV)
Let us therefore come boldly unto the throne of grace, that we may obtain mercy, and find grace to help in time of need.

God is not a genie where we only come to Him to make a wish. We bring everything before Him because He is our Father who cares for our NEEDS and we need to do it without any restrictions, fear or doubt and He will help us see it through. God is doing it in my life and in the lives of many others. I know He can do it for anyone else who is willing to take the step. All it takes is ONE step to get to the NEXT and before you know it, you have reached your goal and passed it, and you are moving onto the next goal. We GO to get somewhere, just to go again. That's what living is all about: being on the MOVE! We can still be on the move when we are being still; but steadily feeding our spirit, mind, body and soul. We may not be physically moving but spiritually moving. It takes moving in the mind first before the rest follows.

Entry 9

My baseline and how much I need with my credit records, all my account balances and standing debt is about $110,000. Now that is just my baseline. If I were to ask my husband, there probably wouldn't be a number because what he wants is innumerable. But it doesn't hurt to ask. I then asked my husband Eric and I was wrong. He actually gave me a number and he also said how he would use it. This is the number Eric came up with, $1,000,000.

I am blessed to earn the kind of money I have. It didn't use to be this way. In fact, I have made more money in the last three years than I have ever made working in all my previous jobs. I thank God for it all and I believe He will give me what I ask for, granting that I continue to play my part in it.

When I surrendered my life to the Lord, He didn't only save me but saved my pockets from wasting money on foolish things that were unhealthy for me spiritually, mentally, and physically.

Months ago, I checked my credit score for free with creditkarma.com and it was at a 720. Then, I applied for a credit card and it brought it below the good mark. Lexington Laws website shows that 690 is good but 750 is better. I was almost at the better mark until I applied for a home loan and the credit card. When I applied for the credit card and the home loan, it placed a hard inquiry on my credit. For those of you who don't know, my loan applications dropped at least five points for each credit inquiry off my FICO Scores. It still didn't add up to me and I realized it was because I had applied earlier this year for a home loan, so basically it was like I applied for two home loans and a credit card. I am giving it a few months before I go back and try again. Incidentally, I was qualified for a loan both times but the home I wanted was above the amount of the loan.

Another thing I've learned is that if you have a credit card, it is wise to call them and find out when they send their reports to the credit bureaus. Making payments on time does not necessarily mean that they get cleared right away from the credit bureau. Finding out when the credit card company submit their reports will help determine when you can and should use your credit card again.

One good tip I can give you is to only use 20% of the amount of the credit you have been given. This will help boost your credit but also make it more affordable to pay back. The last time I checked my credit score was back in September and we are now in November as to the time I am writing this book. I will check it again next year in March 2018 and hopefully my credit score will have gone up higher than the highest it has ever been. However, I will be looking again for our home at the beginning of the year in those areas I have asked God for. This will be another huge goal my family will accomplish.

As I get our numbers in order, investments and savings will also be in the works. I have an idea of what I want to do as far as savings. So far, I have already stopped using one of my credit cards and need to finish off the payments for that one. I am still paying off a school loan which I pray could just be forgiven. LOL! Or I can make $110,000 that I asked for and have it payed off in a few months, unless I raise it to $120,000. This will allow me to take care of my school loan and consolidate my husband's debts, and knock them out all at once.

We have a daughter who is in her first year at Washington State University. Making that amount or having that would help our daughter tremendously. If both my husband and I could make more than we are currently bringing home, we can help pay for our daughter's tuition and fees. She wouldn't have to worry about getting Financial Aid to go to school and ending up like me and most people who go to college who are still paying on their loans.

This can take years, but with prayer, hope, dedication, and consistency it will not be long and my loan will be paid in full. Thank You Jesus!

I am creating a new plan of strategy on how to better handle not only our finances but our time; for time is money. We all have been given the same amount of time in a day. But if you are like me in how I have not been using my time wisely lately, then now is the time to change that. Most of us were taught to save money, but how about saving our time? We never really think about saving time but we always hear people say, "Time is money." So why can't we save time? God is working on me with this.

I feel great knowing where my family stand financially and to have it written out so I can visually see it.

Habakkuk 2:2 (ESV)
And the Lord answered me: Write the vision; make it plain on tablets, so he may run who reads it.

This will help me envision it coming to pass. My prayer is for God to give me the plans and strategies on how to do all these and what initial steps I need to make. Send me the help Lord and make known to me the resources available for me and let the Holy Spirit in me know and discern those individuals You will be sending my way. I pray I am where I need to be and positioned to where You can do all these for me. I pray Lord, that You take anything and anyone out of my life that is not part of this plan You have set out for me to do. Let me be aligned with the right godly people, even with the unbelievers who are watching me and what You are doing in my life that will open their eyes to see that You are a Real True Living God, in Jesus' mighty name, Amen.

Write down all your baseline numbers that include your credit records, account balances, and standing debt. You will need this to be clear about what it is you need.

_____

_____

_____

_____

_____

_____

_____

How do you feel now that you know where you stand
and how much you need to pray/ask God for?

_____

_____

_____

_____

_____

Remember, we have to do our part as well after we
bring it before the Lord. We must make some goals
(short/long term) and the plans we must take to
accomplish those goals. It is in the making for the
taking!!!

For the Bible tells us in James 2:17 that faith without works is dead.

Entry 10

Now that I have my numbers, the actions I am willing to take in order to have the BEST harvest yet starts with changing my mindset about how I see wealth. I will no longer look at money as if it is evil and that someone like me cannot keep it and grow it. I will look at it from my new pair of eyes that sees money as a seed to plant in so many places and to watch it grow, whether it is up close or far away. But I will continue to water it until I cannot water any longer. I want to see a garden full of different plants with all different purposes because it is limitless when God is involved. He wants to multiply not only in my life but in the lives of others who want to grow and live fruitful life in abundance. I will not only invest in myself with the continuous wealth of knowledge and resources I receive, but also invest financially for the future of my children and their children's children, and so forth. I will restart on my savings by giving God His 10% first and then paying myself 10% of each paycheck, from my investor (job). I will open an account and commit to depositing my 10%

for my family's future. I am looking into investing in some stocks not only for my family but for the children, the next generation in the Mausali bloodline, and generations after that. My God, You have not created me or any other human being to stay mediocre. The spirit in us hungers for more and we look to the wrong things to feed that hunger but it's the hunger of creation inside, which You have placed in us. We are Your creation and You have hidden within us many ideas to create things that are profitable, not only monetary but spiritually, mentally, and physically. As Jeremiah 23:3 says: "Then I Myself will gather the remnant of My flock out of all the countries where I have driven them and bring them back to their pasture, and they will be fruitful and multiply." See, some of us have been driven to other places and paths in our lives because of the decisions and circumstances that took place. But when we open our eyes to the truth, we can and will be fruitful to multiply. Genesis 1:28 And God blessed them; and God said to them, "Be fruitful and multiply, and fill the earth, and subdue it; and rule over the fish of the sea and over the birds of the sky and over every living thing that moves on the earth." God has given us the blessings to do our part in the world, to become great and do great things. When He told us this, He was talking about creating life with the things He has given us and to produce more of it, then we can enjoy the circle of life. This doesn't mean to create things in abundance that results to death, like this world is showing us through everything we see and hear nowadays. This world likes to create things at the expense of the lives of others. But God is a loving God and He loves us that much. He gave His only begotten Son, that whosoever believes in Him should not perish, but have everlasting life. God planted His Son, who sacrificed His life, so that many more seeds (people) can grow in Him and have everlasting life. Whether it's our last day on this planet or not, everything big or small we have created that has impacted history will still live on. I am choosing to leave my imprint in this world and have fun while doing it.

What actions are you willing to take now that you know your numbers?

_____

_____

_____

_____

_____

As you imagine your future and see that the plans you have created with God are being met, write down all the great ideas you will be planting for later to get the BEST harvest.

_____

_____

_____

_____

_____

_____

Entry 11

It feels so good to know that I have everything My Father in Heaven has set aside for me. I don't have to wait for anyone's approval, for God has already told me what to do in His Word. I am not saying I have arrived in that place of perfection, but I have arrived in this season to flourish in the gift of writing He has placed within me. I don't have to sit in a room wondering about what's coming because John 14:12 (NLT) says: "I tell you the truth, anyone who believes in me will do the same works I have done, and even greater works." So, that tells me greater is coming but when I look within myself, GREATER is already HERE!!! Because He lives within me. I just have to walk in the greatness.

I visited with a good friend and my sister in Christ, Fia Tasi Taito. We talked about the goodness of our Heavenly Father and what He has done in our lives, and continues to do. The thing I heard throughout our visit was "obedience." She had to remind me that "believing" is exactly that. She also shared with me the word "commitment" that God gave her. This is something many of us mothers struggle with at times: working a full-time job, and finding time to spend with our family and ministry. We try to find a balance, but God is the balance we need. Without Him, we will burn out so fast, and then we will be no good to anyone or ourselves. He gives us the grace and strength to carry on. We just need to do our part to stay connected to the Power Source who gives us ALL the resource we need to do what He has set out for us to do. This visit was not just a regular visit like we thought.

Isaiah 55:8-9 (NIV) says: "For my thoughts are not your thoughts, neither are your ways my ways," declares the Lord. God has bigger plans in the making; we are part of His plan in making things come to pass, whatever that assignment is. This is a season of greatness that is taking place, for "greater" is coming. The song by Jekalyn Carr, "Greater is Coming" just came to my mind right now. This is one of the praise and worship songs that I listen to, and I just realized how aligned this is to what I said earlier in this entry, GREATER is

HERE! Greater is coming and greater is here are like two people designed to meet but they are the same person. They are just in different seasons. When the appointed time comes where they will meet and collide, an explosion of greatness will take place. Just knowing that I have all the resources I need, which is God, I believe without a doubt that He opens the doors to make all things happen. When we truly BELIEVE (OBEY) nothing is impossible for God. He is not a man that He would lie. When we BELIEVE (OBEY), nothing can stand in our way. We may have a couple bumps in the road but it is nothing we cannot handle with God on our side. If God is for us, then who can be against us? God is omnipresent and majestic and no one can contain Him. When we think of the things above, meaning having the mind of Christ, we should know and operate in ALL He has given us. From now on, I am just going for it all. Of course, I will seek God in it all. This includes starting that business and continuing to do the research and studies I need to learn to prepare me for the place where God is taking me next. When we say yes and amen, OMG! The overflow is so much that anyone who is around the outpour will get some of it because that is how great and awesome our God is. If you don't know that, I pray you will make the time to seek Him for yourself. Try Him and see if He will not do it for you. But let's not get it twisted; God is not a genie. You have to align yourself with His will, and then will you reap the benefits of a child of The King.

As you see the limits fall off your life, write down how you feel and what you are going to do to address it. What will you do?

_____

_____

_____

_____

_____

_____

_____

Entry 12

I have put off completing quite a few things God has called me to do. The first thing was completing the 2nd book, this book, before the year 2017 was over. In the middle of the year I was thinking about starting a business and I was doing all the research about it but then I put it in the back burner like the other things. I have been getting this unction to post things on a consistency but not sure whether it's supposed to be a Facebook Live video, Periscope, message, or word of encouragement. I know to me it may look like much but then I remember that God gives each person what they can handle at the level they are at. I don't need to look at the next person because that will be too overwhelming and may even discourage me. Catherine Storing, my Writing Mama would ask, "How do you eat an elephant?" The answer is one bite at a time. Also, I remember having a conversation with one of my sisters in Christ and she reminded me that before we can move onto the next thing, we must complete what God has assigned to us first. I should know this right? But we are human and sometimes we forget, then God places someone in front of us to remind us. He knows what we need and how to redirect our attention back to the assignment when it looks like we are getting off course. I am grateful and thankful to God for all those whom He places in my life to help remind me to stay the course when it seems like I'm drifting.

I'm not saying we can't multitask, but we need to keep our focus on the task at hand and do all we can to complete it. During that visit I had with Fia, we shared much with each other in the little time we had. I am sure we could have gone on and on for hours. That is just how good our God is. He is a good, good Father and He loves us so much. He does not want to see us living beyond our means and beneath who He made us to be.

In our time of sharing, we were strengthening, encouraging, and motivating each other. Those are the kind of visits and fellowships I love. It's like we are recharging off of each other and I don't leave drained. Thank You Lord for the Body of Christ!

We have heard this saying, "It's a small world." But the opportunities are vast out there and it's just waiting for us to grab it and run with it. Who cares if someone else is doing it? No one can do it like you. There is something you can give that the next business or person cannot. It is up to us to expand our territories. This is only a small world when we limit ourselves in our thinking.

I have no excuses to not complete any of the things God has called me to do. My coworker blessed me with a Planner so I can keep my appointments and show up on time. Thank you Rovila! As far as checking in with our Heavenly Father and making sure what I am doing is aligned with His will, I have nothing to worry about but to do it. Plus, worry don't do anyone any good, and it's a sin. I don't want to make a move without hearing from God first. Sometimes we get caught up making moves and expect God to meet us there; but if He didn't tell us to move, then we end up reaping the repercussions of the aftermath. Other times we use waiting on God as an excuse too, to not take that leap of faith and step He is waiting on us to take. While God is waiting on us, we are waiting for a confirmation from Him and additional confirmations to follow. We become blind to the signs because we are either hoping God will change His mind about what we thought He was telling us; or because we are waiting for the "big bang" confirmation. God is saying to us, the "big bang" you are waiting on will take place only when you step out. He is telling us to come the same way He instructed Peter in Matthew 14. In this story, Jesus calls Peter to step out of the boat and into the water. But when Peter saw the wind, he got scared and began to sink, and then he cried out to Jesus. Of course, Jesus was there to catch him like older siblings do. He then asked Peter, "Why did you doubt?" He is saying to us: "I know that what I'm asking you to do may look impossible and scary but I AM here." He is saying to us, "I know that where I am asking you to go is somewhere you are not familiar with and the people may not accept you, but trust Me. When it looks like things are coming your way and you don't know what to do, come to Me." Some things may come to distract you and discourage you like the wind did when Peter took his eyes off Jesus. He is saying, "I will be there walking it out with you and I will be there to pick you up, but you must know and believe you have everything you need to keep going because I have given it ALL to you." When you complete the assignment I have given you, the assignment you thought was impossible for someone like you to complete, then will you know and be able to say, "Truly I am a child of God!" You will look back and see I was there with you the whole time. I Am the Beginning and the End, the Alpha and the Omega. Therefore, whatever you do, seek Me first in it all and I will help you see it to the end. You will have the kind of peace this world cannot give you.

You have NOTHING holding you back. You have EVERYTHING you need. You have access to all the tools, resources, and connections to do what God has called you to finish. What are you going to do with the harvest and how are you going to use it?

Write down what you will pursue now with everything you have inside of you that you have been putting off because of fear and the thoughts of not having enough.

_____

_____

_____

_____

_____

_____

_____

_____

_____

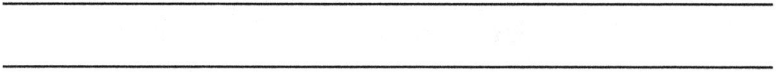

Section Three
Saving & Investing Like a Boss

Entry 13

So many things were going through my mind today. I got up, prayed, read a bit, and then laid in bed thinking about what this day was going to bring. My sister Sonya came by to pick up my daughter Uriah, niece Deejra and I. We were going with her to the church where my other sister, Patsy, attends. She was dedicating her son, Iopu (Job), and celebrating his 2nd birthday. I didn't know what to expect at this service. I prayed in the sanctuary before it started and asked the Holy Spirit to touch the hearts of all who were there and to let that Sunday be like no other. Everything from the beginning to the end came out awesome. The praise and worship was amazing. The message was life changing for those who had the ears to hear what the Lord was saying. The Pastor talked about resurrection and what it means. His message was preparing the people for the upcoming Sunday as they will be conducting baptisms that day.

Though I had so much to do, my mind was focused on the service. I had things to do at home, at work, writing assignments, and preparations for my daughter's 16th neon dance birthday party. I haven't sent the music playlist to the DJ or studied for my exam. This was a "Jesus take this from me day." I made up my mind to enjoy this day and not to think of any of the things on my "To Do" list.

I had a great time with my sister and her family. We witnessed many babies being dedicated at the altar right along with my sister's son. I lost track of time and was running late for my meeting with a friend, but God made a way for us to visit with each other. That visit in itself was another awesome and divine time.

I finally made it home and went straight to writing, which I was behind in. I only have myself to blame: my lack of planning; and my inability to say no to people and situations that will take my time away from finishing my assignments. I recall two things I heard

Tina Moore Brown mentioned on two of her scopes. If you don't know who Tina is, she is part of the Dream Team with Catherine Storing and Pastor Kimberly Jones. They are mighty women of God who are individually different but all have the same heart to help people with the love of God and coach them to become great. I try and catch them on Periscope or Facebook whether they're live or on their replays. Anyways, I never planned my days or weeks like Tina mentioned. After listening to her scope, I made a decision to take my first step by planning my day the night before. As soon as I master that, I can move up to planning out my weeks, then months, and then a year.

I started planning out my days on the index cards laying on my desk, and it just reminded me of Catherine Storing and her love for index cards. I am now getting in the habit of creating these "To Do" list and marking them off complete as I go. If I didn't get a chance to accomplish something, it will be moved on to the next day's "To Do" list and listed accordingly to the order of importance. I know it may seem like something easy to do but if you have never done it, this takes some getting used to. Thank you TMB!

I thank God for His peace that surpasses all human understanding. I didn't feel rushed or anxious but I knew much had to be done. I had God's peace with me. Thinking about what I did two days ago was more like an all day and night run. Thank God for keeping me sane because I almost caught an attitude and was about to get irritated. Of course, that's what happens when I get up at 4 a.m. and run errands until 10:30 p.m. I added on things to my plate I didn't need to. I could have avoided all that by saying a simple "no." I would have been one angry grump if I didn't have God. He seriously carried me through that day and night. God also came to my rescue when I had one of those brown bag moments last month.

Isaiah 41:10 (KJV) says, "Do not fear for I am with you and do not be dismayed for I am your God. I will strengthen you and help you; I will uphold you with my righteous right hand." I almost had a nervous breakdown and I think I was having an anxiety attack at work trying to meet our month end closing. But God said, "Take a deep breath Corina, focus. Get in the zone and you will complete it." I had no time to feel any type of way or get in my emotions. I was now in a zone.

The next day I sat at my desk thinking about what just happened and how I prayed the night before for God to give me rest and let me sleep in His peace. You better believe it, I woke up the next morning energized and well rested. Praise God! He did exactly what His word set out to do. I cried at my desk because month end was over and now I was able to process all that just took place the day before. Thank You God for being an awesome and right on time God! Thank You my Strong Tower and Refuge! Thank You Lord for loving me! I love you Abba Father!!!

Sometimes we can be on a good run and then all of a sudden something out of the blue comes at us. Yes, we are human and can freak out, but we need to know everything will be fine. We need to remember to get in God's face and read His word, praying scriptures over our minds; then, we will be comforted with His peace.

Entry 14

I am very blessed to have many invisible assets I have been taking for granted. I am blessed with the ability to walk spiritually and naturally. Some people can only do one or none. Thank You Lord! Thank You for the vision you have given me to see what's in front of me physically, and to also see spiritually. I am grateful to be able to put a face with a name, whether it is a person place, or thing. Thank You for the ability to see what strongholds look like and how to recognize it when it's in my face or in my life. Thank You Father for Your wisdom; the wisdom You have given me so I would know, understand, and experience Your truth and love like no other. You have blessed me with everything I am and have. I am able to not only enjoy them but also share them with others. Thank you for my sense of humor that is out of this world; I know I got that from You. Just like that song, "She get it from her Mama." I can say, "I got it from my Papa."

As I sit here doing an inventory of the invisible blessings in my life that I may not be aware of, I decided to list some below. Do you know what areas of your life are already rich and wealthy? When you get done reading mine, make a list of your own and see what you come up with.

My Invisible Asset Inventory:

Intelligent

Self-Published Author and Publisher

Motivational

Encourager

Good listener

Organized

Cleanliness

Arm mobility

Zero pills intake

Anxiety Free Life

Roof over my head

A working car paid in full

Great cook

I can cut, color, and braid hair

Nail artist

Crochet

Singer

Giver

Counselor

Teacher

Event Planner/Coordinator

Chauffeur

Write down your invisible assets and how each one has been used in your life. Try to be detailed. You probably will surprise your own self like I did.

_____

_____

_____

_____

_____

_____

Entry 15

From the list I wrote on Entry 14, I decided to put
dollar values next to each blessing of assets. OMG! I am
a very wealthy person. This is the number attached to
those assets with the dollar amount I valued it at
$2, 000, 012, 375, 000.00. Thank you, Jesus! I am a
TRILLIONAIRE!!! My old mindset would have never
thought that those numbers could be associated with
me. I didn't even know how to say that number: 2
trillion, 12 million, 375 thousand dollars. When we
don't know things, we lack. God's plan for us is to
prosper. He says in Hosea 4:6 (KJV): My people are
destroyed for lack of knowledge and He also says in
Psalms 34:10 (KJV)…but those who seek the Lord will
NOT lack any good thing. We never really take into
consideration all the invisible assets we have that others
notice. We don't even look at it as an asset. We just
think it's something we do or we were born naturally to
do, but in actuality they are assets. I don't know how
much you would value any of your assets but the

number I got for just the few I listed came out to be a huge amount.

Why don't we value these assets like we should? These are gifts and talents God has placed in us and we should not ever think we are broke after doing an exercise like this. How can we? How can I? Now, what am I going to do with this information I have just discovered about myself? I am going to put it to use. I can bless so many with it. Freely it was given to me, freely I can also give it. Or, I can also turn it around and offer them as services to the public and make an income out of it. We are always looking for the next best thing outside but we should look within ourselves first. What we are looking for, we can create. We know what we want and how we want it, so why not create it? Let's create wealth! Let's start first by creating a wealthy mindset and wealthy relationships. I'm not saying to only make friends and reach out to the people who have money, but to reach out to others who have wealthy mindsets or those who want to learn how to have a wealthy mindset. Build relationships with them, learning from them in exchange for what you know. I didn't think this was possible, not until now. It is also opening me up and showing me things that I can do as well. Wealth is anything with value; not just money. We hear the saying, "knowledge is power" and "money is power." They go hand in hand. In order for you to have money, you first need to have the knowledge on how to make this money, and the knowledge to keep this money flowing like rivers that don't run dry. What is it that you could do and offer as a service to the public and generate income? There is a need out there and we must find it then create and be the solution to that need. What do you believe your service is worth? For example, if you can't cook anything but you believe you can make the best soup in all of your state, then why not start making soups and sell it? Start off slow and have your friends and family be the taste testers. Ask them which is their favorite and what could use a little more or less of? There you have it! Now the rest is up to you on how you will go about it. What do you have inside of you that needs birthing? Mine is this book and who knows what else? Only God knows!

Entry 16

I am quiet on the outside but a roaring lioness on the inside.

I am cool like a fresh breath of wind blowing leaves in the fall.

I am calm like the deep blue still waters in the summer nights.

I am going to complete this book with the manuscript edited and published by Spring 2018.

I believe the double doors will open for me like Cyrus in Isaiah 45:1.

I believe new relationships will be made as I approach this new stage.

I believe I will be writing my third book and it will be something different from the first and second.

I believe I am moving into a new level, showing up but not arriving; always staying humble.

I see myself helping many because of my books, whether it's the informational content or motivation and inspiration to write one too.

I see revelations, deliverance, and healing taking place for readers as I received mine while writing this.

I see everything I have written in this book coming to pass...

Follow me on my Twitter and Facebook page Author Corina Mausali to see what God is having me create next. Who knows if it's a third book or business, stay tune.

Try creating a verbal declaration to yourself with your newfound wealthy confidence and worth. This is to remind you on those days when you are unsure of who you are and what you were created to do.

Entry 17 & 18

I had to ask myself who is holding me back from becoming the person I know I was created to be. If you guessed me, you are right. The first person I see holding me back is me. I am afraid of jumping out there and really see what I am created to be. I know I have a purpose like everyone else but finding that purpose is where I struggled. I know I am to help people but in what way and where? I tend to offer my services to help in all areas I believe I can assist in, but at the end of the day I am left feeling drained, exhausted, and overworked. I would ask myself, did I do enough? Feeling that I haven't done enough, I would also think that there is not enough time in a day to get everything done. I realize from writing this out that the problem lies right there. I always think that I need to fix and help everyone. What I am only realizing now is that if each one could teach even one person to reach another one, then not many people would need the help like many are desperately seeking. It's like passing a baton in a relay and cheering the next runner to go and keep running, cheering them on until they have crossed the finish line.

We all have our part to play in this relay race called life and to pass the baton of knowledge (wealth) to the next person to create something new for the next person to pick up and learn from. We are God's masterpiece and each one of us are colors to one another's canvass. Some add little colors, some add more, some blend well while others don't; but all in all, we have touched someone in some way and that piece of art now is walking around on display for others to see.

The next person who I say is holding me back would be my husband. It's not like he is not supportive of what I do. He is very supportive in his own way. He is really proud of the person I am becoming but at the same time he feels neglected because I have put my work and ministry before him. This is something God is working on with me. This is the reason why God has me in my sit-in season right now as I am writing this. My husband loves me and tells me I am his beautiful wife, lifetime partner, and best friend. The thing is, he puts me on a pedestal when I don't deserve to be. I have to remind him that I am not perfect, and that God is still working in me. I am trying to be someone better than who I thought I was and who he saw me as. I am saved and my husband is not. My prayer to God is for my husband to become saved and have a close relationship with God than he has with me. I want him to know what it's like to have a relationship with God and to see His hand move in our lives like I do. I pray for his salvation. Because he is an unbeliever, I think that is also a hindrance in my journey. I believe God is working in him. I see how we are such a powerful team when we were not saved, so I can see how more powerful we can be together for the Kingdom of God. I don't know what else to say but I pray God will continue to work on us both and help us both in and through this. May God send righteous and godly people to my husband where ever he goes, whether it's at his work site, the grocery store, or gas station, and that they will sow seeds and water them in the name of Jesus. I pray for God to soften his heart to be in acceptance of the godly things, and that he will one day soon join me either in a Sunday service or an event I may attend as well in Jesus' mighty name, Amen.

Real FREEDOM is TAKEN, NOT asked for. What or who is holding you back from becoming who YOU KNOW you are created to be? Be true in what you come up with and write them down.

_____

_____

_____

_____

_____

_____

_____

_____

_____

Entry 19

I am so ready to leave the struggle bus behind. Last year around Thanksgiving, my sister and I went down to Lake Hamilton Bible Camp in Hot Springs, Arkansas and many spiritual chains I was carrying fell off of me during that visit. I went back again earlier February of this year while in the midst of writing my first book, "Your Will Be Done 30 Day Devotions." Again, more chains were falling off and I left there with such confidence that I was no longer picking up or attaching myself to those things that were just broken off of me. That was part of my struggle and I didn't realize that it was somehow attached to everything I did. Something happened to my sister and I spiritually when we took that first step of faith purchasing those roundtrip tickets to Arkansas, to a place we have never been to and where we didn't know anyone. Upon us leaving the camp site from our first visit, my sister took another step of faith and booked us a room for the upcoming Women's Conference in February. It was at that moment we knew we were coming back with no questions asked. We didn't know any one at this camp except for God and He was the One who led our every step there. This is the same thing He is doing with me in writing this second book. I no longer struggle with making ends meet like before; and if I do, it's not really a struggle and it's nothing I can't conquer because God is with me. It is by His Power and Might that I can do what I do. I have already decided to restart my savings again by tithing to God and paying myself. On top of that, I just invested in a few stocks and I am feeling pretty good where I am right now. I am willing to cut out spending money like I have been or known to spend. I need to be more strict and consistent on how we as a family are managing our finances. I have been doing research on things I believe God wants me to put together to help others get to the finish line. Also, it will be another source of income for my family. He is using another one of the many gifts He has placed in me. I can start putting a price on my services because time is money and we can never get that time back once it's gone. The goal here is to save money and make money at the same time and how are we going to go about it and what are we going to do to accomplish that?

Recently, I had a conversation with my husband about us not spending any more like before and that we are going to have to tighten up because the plans God has for His children are to prosper, have a hope and a future, and not to be wasteful with the blessings He has and continues to give us. We need to develop saving habits and key tools to experience freedom like we dream and hope for. If we start now before the year ends, this will be the best decision we will make. Not only will we finish 2017 strong by staying focused and committed to the goal and task at hand, but we will be walking into 2018 with our heads held up high. God is doing a new thing. By making the decision to change our mindset, God will use this renewed mind to get us to our New, Now, and Next level of blessings.

Are you ready to leave the struggle bus behind? How is your savings game? What are you willing to do in order to save? Write down your thoughts, truths, and revelations that come up.

_____

_____

_____

_____

_____

_____

_____

_____

If you need a way to save automatically, you can check out SmartyPig. It's a great way to schedule your savings habit.

Section Four
Expanding My Money Mindset

Entry 20

I am sitting here thinking about this question I am not sure how to answer. Have I confused head knowledge with faith knowledge? What I do know is this: God promised to change me and He understands I am a work in progress until the day He comes for me. Even though I am still growing into the person He has created me to be, I will not give up because He abides in me. It is for that very reason why I can't give up. It's not in Him to give up. He didn't give up when He took the cross for us in Calvary. I will not and refuse to give up. He gives me the strength to keep going even when some days I don't feel like it. God has brought me too far to just throw in the towel now or at any time for that matter. I will remain committed to the process NOT because of what I have learned so far about my money story but it's because of the faith knowledge that drives me forward every day. This why I am willing to stay committed to rewriting my money story process until it matches what God says about my future. Did I expect my money story to change the moment I learned why it was messed up? Yes. But drastically, no. It takes time and planning to come up with strategies on what to do and how to deal with issues that may occur dealing with our finances. Since I learned why, what, and who it was messing up my opportunity of becoming wealthy, I had to come to a realization that this is not working for me. I made a conscious choice to no longer do the things in that will take from my future, my families, or the future of those who I want to reach out to. In order for those who I want to help become successfully wealthy, I need to learn how to become and live that way first in all areas of my life. Sharing the success is such a reward, especially when we can teach each other how to become successfully wealthy. Yes, we are individually different and not all our steps and ways may work for everyone, but we must at least start first by making a conscious decision to say, "No more am I going to live that kind of life with a poverty mindset that has kept me bound for so long." As we grow to become whom God created us to be, we will find out what works for us and what doesn't. Only then can we share with others our experiences that will show them how we are able to be in the position we are in: spiritually, mentally, physically, and financially. Being on top is lonely, with no one to share the beautiful view. This is why God created us for one another, to lift each other up and show one another that we too can do it! What conscious decision do you need to make today in your life to change your money story? For we are all responsible for our own destiny and where we are headed. It all starts with an idea and a choice to decide what we are going to do next and move on it.

Write down why are you still struggling.

_____

_____

_____

_____

If you KNOW better, then why are you still struggling?

_____

_____

_____

_____

_____

Could it be that you have confused your knowledge with faith knowledge? Head knowledge is good but faith knowledge is so much better and greater. Faith knowledge is knowing the promises of God and what He will do for you and what He is doing on your behalf even though you are still under His construction of who you are being molded to be. Having faith knowledge should move you forward EVERY day.

Entry 21

There are many reasons why I keep getting up, learning, and showing up. One of the reasons is because I can't, will not, and refuse to stay on the ground when and if I fall. I know I no longer have to be this strong person for everyone. I can be who God created me to be and that's being the woman who has the love of God for people, but not with the false humility. I am grateful and thankful to God for the gift of discernment to know I can have love for the people and that I can't help everyone. I keep getting up because I look at the eyes of my family and I'm doing it for them like my parents did for me and my siblings. I do it because I know there is more out there for me to do in this life, the life that God has blessed me with. I keep getting up for those who I know is out there looking for answers like I was and not knowing who to go to. I may not be the sharpest tool in the shed but I know what I have experienced and by sharing it could help the next person. Recently I had a conversation with my coworker about learning. We talked about us both attending some form of schooling to learn something new. He is going to school for Accounting/Finances, which is the department we work in and I attend Holy Spirit University for ministry. I told him there is so much to learn and we don't know everything. When we think we know everything, at that moment we just stopped learning. That puts a stumbling block for us to learn more and to become something other than that mediocre person no one will remember. I am here to leave a legacy behind and when I do leave this earth my story will live on. Words have meanings and so do names. My father's last name is Mausali, the same name on this book which means rock solid. As my Heavenly Father is my Rock of Ages, my natural father is my rock who kept me solid. Coincidence? I don't think so. There is no coincidence with God. I keep showing up because if I don't, who will show up for me or anyone else in my family? I keep showing up because I trust God is doing something and bringing me through it. This is too deep for my immediate family to even dig in. I'm doing it for those of the Samoan culture. We, Samoans, have a strange way of doing things and many of the things that take place in our lives we don't talk about. It's almost like bad juju. So, we don't get to really express ourselves and especially as children, we had no place or room to talk. What a child had to say was and is not important or at least that's what most of the elders and some in my generation believe. This is why I turned to writing and now God has made it a way for me to reach others. Learning and reading is something I really enjoy doing. My sisters would crack jokes about me and my many degrees and certificates. My mom even said to me once, "The world is going to end and you are still going to school." That was her way of telling me to come to her prayer meetings and draw myself closer to God. Funny thing is I responded to my mom, "What makes you think I'm not closer to God than you all because I don't come to your meetings?" From there, God used the pride in me to push me to spend even more time with Him than I ever had. God knew what He was doing when He had my mom ask me that because He knew what it was going to take for me to move. What is God telling you to move on to? It's not too late to come to God if you haven't truly given yourself to Him. What better place to do it, if you haven't done it? Right here and right now, where you are. If you want to do it now, all you have to do is read the prayer below out loud with a genuine heart.

Dear Lord,

I admit that I am a sinner. I have done many things that don't please you. I have lived my life for myself. I am sorry and I repent. I ask you to forgive me. I believe that you died on the cross for me and rose three days later, to save me. You did what I could not do for myself. I come to you now and ask you to take control of my life; I give it to you. Help me to live every day in a way that pleases you. I love you, Lord, and I thank you that I will spend all eternity with you, in Jesus' name. Amen.

Now that you have said that prayer, it's time to get up. Dust yourself off, open up the Holy Bible and learn the Word of God for yourself and show up to the things God is calling you to and watch Him show out for you. Will you sit back on the bleachers and cheer everyone else on or will you get in the race and run to the finish line? It's time to change the game and re-write your story. Yes, I have fallen down many times but I kept getting back up. Don't be so hard on yourself. This time, try it from a different angle or approach. You are learning and doing something new and it's different. It may take a few tries but what matters is that you keep getting up and keep pushing forward.

Entry 22

If I could name a few things that I am willing to surrender to God NOW, even if I were having a hard time doing so, it will be my position at my work place as a Major Account Specialist for our Accounts Receivable Department. Although I am willing to surrender it up willingly, I don't believe God will allow me to because He has me there for a reason. When the position was first offered to me, I thought to myself, "Why are they offering this job to me? Can I even do this job?" I know the God I serve and I know the prayers I prayed but this was so suddenly. And around that time, the word many were speaking was, God is going to do the Suddenlies -- the all of a sudden kind of things. Well, this so happened to be one of those sudden things. I didn't even have to apply for this position. They offered it to me and gave me some time to think about it. They offered a certain amount of pay and after a few days of negotiations we came to an agreement on a reasonable amount. I have been in this position since the beginning of this year and it is now December. What I thought I couldn't do then, I am doing it now. God will never give us anything to do if He didn't believe we could do it. Part of getting this position meant I had to have a talk with myself. This is something we all do in our lives. Whether we are talking ourselves into something or talking ourselves out of something. Majority of the time we talk ourselves out of something when we let fear cripple us. When we allow these fears in, we also allow it to steal our blessings from us. We have to change what we are concentrating and meditating on.

I remember the first position they offered me. When they showed me the amount of pay, I was like, "Let me think about it and I will get back to you." Mind you, if this was the old me, I would have hopped right on the offer with no hesitation. But I am a new creation in Christ Jesus and He said, ask and you shall receive. When I went back to speak with them, I asked if we could do something about the pay. They said, "What do you have in mind?" I had a higher number in mind; they came with a lower number. But something in me said,

"Go for the middle number." When I told them what I am willing to take, they said they will get back to me. Three days later they agreed with my number and that's when I told them I will take the position. Before I even went in to make the negotiation about the pay, fear tried to creep in. I had to talk to myself and recite 2 Timothy 1:7 and Matthew 7:7. I was concentrating on the Word of God and standing on the promises that I know, that I know when I ask, I will receive, and I will go in confidently because it is through Christ that I can, the One who strengthens me. I didn't concentrate on, "What if they said no?" I didn't meditate on the negative. My mind was set on, "I'm going to do this and there is nothing else to it." I would have been more upset with myself if I didn't ask and then have it in the back of mind, "What if I had only asked?" I had to surrender that fear and anxiety to God. That was one of the situations I brought to Him. Since being at this workplace, most of the things I have gone through have all been learning lessons. I believe I have more to learn before He releases me. I am also willing to give up all the time I have, to spend it with Him like I had a couple times before. I am having a hard time doing this because of my unbalanced time management with my job in the corporate world. I am trying to marry my vocation with my calling; but the reason I can't do it is because I am trying. If I gave it over to God completely, I wouldn't have to try and do anything except to listen and obey to what He is saying. It's when we try and do things by ourselves that we get in our own way and in God's way from doing what He needs to do to get us to that place He has prepared for us. I am willing to surrender it all; the house, car, job, family, and myself. God knows us better than we think. It's like He does the opposite of what we want. I'm not saying that He wouldn't give us what we want, but He knows the perfect time of when to give us what we think we may want at that specific time. God is an "On Time God" and He is perfect in every way. He knows the time for everything. If He left it up to us, we will be late for almost everything and too early for most of the things. It will not turn out right because we would have missed the connection for the divine and appointed time to do such things. I want to do what God has called me to do and that means not being preoccupied with issues WAY above my pay grade. God is in control so I must let Him lead the way, for He knows it better than me. He is the Way, the Truth, and the Life.

Do you go to a negative place EVERY time you get an unexpected curve ball? Do you think God was surprised by it? He knows what we go through and what we may have to face. Sometimes He prepares us, but we get so caught up in our own self that we miss the signs and warnings. Either way we choose, God still has an answer and a way out. Some answers may cause some hurt and pain but it will only be for a little bit and at least we will know from our experience what not to do and what to do next. We will also know what that will look like the next time we are faced with the same situation.

What are you willing to surrender to God? If you are having a hard time doing so, tell Him. He wants to hear it personally from you.

_____

_____

_____

_____

_____

What are you going through that you can bring to God now? Is it fear and anxiety, if so from what and can you surrender it to God?

_____

_____

_____

_____

_____

_____

Entry 23

Dear Papa,

First, I want to apologize for treating you the way I have been these past few months. I have been quickly checking in with you and then getting caught back up in being busy with the cares of this world.

From time to time I wonder why I go back and forth like that with You. But, I don't have any excuses why I do it. I can say because I have so much to do but it still doesn't give me an excuse to not spend the time I need to spend with You. Then when I realize I'm doing it, I'm back to crying and asking You for Your forgiveness.

Why do I do it? Why do I busy myself when I know being busy is an acronym for B=Being, U=Under, S=Satan's and Y=Yoke. And I know what You have for me is WAY better than anything this world could offer me.

Help me Father to manage my time wisely. Give me Your wisdom to know what to take on and what not to. Help me to plan out my days to be on time with You and everything else You need me to do.

I want and need to get back to that place I was with You when I first came to know You, but even more deeper than that. HELP ME PAPA!!! I want and need to be so in tune with You that I could even hear You in my sleep; help me to know how beneficial it is for me to stay close and having that intimate relationship with You. Help me to find balance in what I am doing and prune and take away all the things that are not of You or that doesn't profit Your Kingdom.

Your Daughter,

Corina

I wrote that letter because I knew how my relationship with God was and where it should be. He is the Creator of the ENTIRE world and He controls everything. He gives to us so we can give to others. We are not here for ourselves, He created us for one another. How can we justify our current financial situation when our relationship with God is not where it should be? He is the One who gives the increase and opens the doors of opportunities for us. He gives the seed to the sower. If we even think about wanting to be wealthy God's way, (which is more everlasting spiritually, mentally, and physically) then we need to restore our relationship with Him. We need to seal it airtight.

Why don't you take this time to write a letter to God and let Him know how you will go about fixing your relationship with Him.

_____

_____

_____

_____

Entry 24

Today in the midst of all the things that are going on in my life, I think about all the victories You, Lord have brought Your people through, and the many obstacles they overcame because of You.

How you brought the victory to the people of Israel through David, defeating the giant Goliath with a sling shot and a stone. And Abraham's 318 trained servants who fought against the Armies of Shinar and defeated them who took his nephew Lot and all his goods.

I also remember how the Jewish people were saved from being killed when You placed Esther on the throne as Queen to stand in the gap for the people. And how You protected the three Hebrew boys in the furnace for not worshipping no other god or king but You.

Today I am choosing to celebrate early. I am making a declaration:

I know who I am and whose I am. I will not let any situations or circumstances take the blessings God has given me from this day forward. Psalm 3:8 says victory belongs to the Lord and Your blessings is upon Your people. My Daddy is a shield for me. He is my Glory and the One who lifts my head. (Psalm 3:3) When I lay down to sleep and wake back up (Psalm 3:5) it is Him who keeps me. Enemy, you may think you're getting away with something by messing with me; but you didn't know that I am the child of the Most High King. I am not afraid of you, and My Daddy is going to strike (Psalm 3:7) all my enemies on the cheekbone and break their ungodly teeth, you have been warned.

Come up with your own victory declaration and give the enemy his eviction notice.

_____

_____

_____

_____

Entry 25

It's about that time of the year where many people will be spending their time and money in this madness of Christmas mayhem. I do not partake in these holiday rushes. I used to be one of the many consumers who would go crazy spending all my money and time away from home just to make that money to spend for Christmas and every major holiday the US recognizes. But what was revealed to me back in 2012 was the last time I celebrated any holidays or bought anything for Christmas. Actually, I believe that was the year we started not to celebrate Christmas. I believe in Christ and that He was born, but I am not into the way everyone else celebrates it. It was hard being around my family since they still celebrated it like the rest of the world. They still celebrate it to this very day but it's to each their own and their beliefs. I have my reasons why I don't. Since then, I have been able to save more money during all these holidays and I am not running around stressed and overwhelmed because of it either. I don't believe I should wait for this one day to buy someone a gift when I can do it throughout the year. Some get confused when I tell them I don't celebrate it because it doesn't make sense to them when they know I believe in God. I am all for the family gatherings and if it was up to me, I would do it a whole week instead of just one day. The thing is, the gifts we give each other should be what we can do for one another. Yes, having a store-bought gift is nice but someone doing something nice for someone else is truly amazing. It's because of the gift God has placed in you that you are able to share with others the way I am sharing with you through this book. This is a true act of kindness that cannot be bought. I choose to celebrate the birth of my Lord and Savior every day. I don't want to get in a debate about Jesus' birthday not being on December 25th. I am grateful He was born and that He came to die for our sins and rose again so we can have this opportunity to come before God like Jesus has and does. But that's me. Since this is the season of sales too, I used to go shopping just because I could and I wouldn't waste my time wrapping the items up. I would just hand them out. But even then, that was still me participating in what I didn't need to do, especially if I was trying to save and invest instead of self-soothing myself with all these temporary things that will lose its value anyways. But if I were to purchase something right now, I would purchase my family a home and another car. If I could get those right now, those two would be the best gifts I would be receiving physically in 2017 besides publishing my first book. I know everything has its time. I am waiting for the right time, which is God's time. Purchasing our home and another vehicle is a legitimate investment for my family and future self indeed. Believe me, when this does take place, I will be doing the ugly cry like I always do when God blesses me in such a way that I can't even make any sense of it. Just being in that "awe" moment with Him is already overwhelming. This is something we have been waiting to do for a while now and because God will bless us with it, I will use it to bless others. For what He gives us we are to share. I am excited to see God do it for us in 2018. Thank You Papa for doing it and moving on our behalf, in Jesus' mighty name. Thank You for the best gift of all, the gift of salvation through Your Son Jesus. For everything I have and will receive, truly is a gift from You.

Why do you buy the things you want to buy for yourself and others? Are you investing or just spending?

_____

_____

_____

_____

_____

What are you trying to buy with your gifts that only Jesus can give you?

_____

_____

_____

_____

_____

We should always ask ourselves before making any purchases, "Is this an investment or am I just trying to fill a void that only Jesus can fill?" This will help us not be wasteful with our time and finances. I would ask myself whenever I was going to purchase something if it was a need or a want. If it was a need I would get it, but if it was a want then I wouldn't, unless I had extra to spend. But then after I get it, I wouldn't even really use it. I just got it because I could and wanted it. Now that is just greedy. And we all know that greed is a sin. Thank God I no longer do that and thank God for His forgiveness of my sin. We are humans and we make mistakes. The thing is to acknowledge our mistakes and learn from it, especially if we consider ourselves to be children of God. We strive to become perfect and always show ourselves approved unto God, not being ashamed, and rightly dividing God's Word, which is the Truth.

Entry 26

Crazy how the question of the day is, "To shop or not to shop?" Well, to be honest, I have gone shopping twice before even writing this entry. My cousin's baby just turned two and my friend's daughter just turned three. I was unable to make it to my cousin's baby's party because of class, but I told him I would drop something off for her. So, that is exactly what I did. I went shopping and I dropped off her gift. Then a couple days later my friend told me about her daughter's birthday coming up and I went shopping again. The thing is, when I go shopping for people, I end up buying something for myself as well. Most of the time, it's me buying things I don't really need, but just want because I can. If I am the one responsible for my own future financially and I am the only one who can make the decisions about my future, I need to start nipping these shopping sprees in the bud. I need to not open my mouth to say anything as well like I did with my cousin. I am not saying that I didn't want to buy her anything; the point is, do all these gifts and spending align with the DIRECT goals for my life? Thinking about that question, the answer is no.

When I say I'm going to do something, I do it. I am a person of my word. I know there will be many more birthdays and events that will be coming up and I need to be well prepared on how I can better handle it than I did these last two birthdays. If I do decide to do anything, it better be with things I already have on hand to make or create that's lying around the house so I can save my money towards what I need and will accomplish for my family's future. Not only did I spend money but I also spent time, time that I could have used towards getting things completed and planned out for my next project. I could have gotten the rest that I so needed instead of saying constantly that I'm so tired. I didn't have to get a gift for my friend's daughter. Plus, she didn't even know I was getting her daughter one so why did I feel obligated to buy her a gift? Oh, because she bought my daughter one? Am I trying to please her?

Or my cousin? We know what the word of God says about men pleasers – those individuals who like to please people.

Galatians 1:10(NASB)
For am I now seeking favor of men, or of God? Or am I striving to please men? If I were still trying to please men, I would not be a bond-servant of Christ.

No one has ever died because they didn't get a gift. There were many others that showed up to those parties who brought gifts. So, it wasn't like these two babies were going without. They wouldn't have known if I didn't give them anything. Going back to the point, are these gifts or spending sprees beneficial to my future? No. Then I don't need to be doing this kind of spending, if my goal is to save money and not spend it. I could have used those funds to invest in more stocks or add to the ones I already have. The choices we make today really determines what our tomorrows will bring. From now on, moving forward, I will no longer spend any money on things that do not pertain to the success of my family's future and to stand firm and not let guilt try to creep in. It all starts with our mindset and today I have made up in my mind – NO MORE!!! I will NOT spend and that is the answer to the question of the day. I have a goal and that is to move into our home by Spring of 2018 and I need to save all I can for it and for whatever else may happen unexpectedly.

Since we are on having new mindsets and setting goals to do better and become better, ask yourself the same question. Will these upcoming gifts/donations and spending for birthdays, anniversaries, graduations, girl scouts, and wedding seasons or whatever the occasion may be DIRECTLY align with your life's goals? We can pick our decisions BUT we can't pick our consequences. The choice is always ours to make.

Entry 27

I have been playing myself very small and short changing myself from the things God has given me. He has His arms stretched out handing the things over to me, but I keep looking around and stretching myself out, trying to do it all by myself when God has given it to me. He's saying, "What are you doing my child, I have done it all for you? I need you to just walk in it and reach out towards Me to grab the blessings. I have your name written all over. That doesn't mean take what I have given you and forget who gave it to you and run with it like you don't know any better. Remember, just as I give it; I can take it away."

Father in the name of Jesus, I ask You for Your forgiveness for thinking I can do it by myself and that I needed to do it by myself. Forgive me for asking for Your help and then getting in Your way and my own, by trying to control things when You are the one who is in control. Forgive me for not letting You have full control in all the areas of my life. Lord, I repent of my sins and thank You Lord for Your forgiveness. Thank You for Your heavenly angels You have assigned to me to guide me in the way I should go according to the plans You have created for my life in Jesus' mighty name.

Lord I believe in all the things You say, can, and will do. I trust Lord You are who You say You are. There is no doubt in my mind that You are the One and Only True Living God. There is no one I know of or have read of in the Bible that You have touched and were not transformed. Any time You crossed their paths there was an immediate change or transformation of some sort for their good. I don't know how anyone could read the Bible and not be moved by the words that created all things and continue to create. Here is my plea to You.

Father God, in the name of Jesus, I come before You with this plea. I am asking for the life You have designed specifically for me and I need You every step of the way. You have been with me, creating the first book like You are with me creating this one. This is part of Your plan, but there are other things as well. Lord, You know I am in the process of purchasing my home and You also have a project in me that I need to complete. I am going to need some assistance and I know the assistance will come when I go through the project. Lord, I ask for a huge home with a beautiful back yard with good soil to grow things in. Let the purchasing process of our home be what I am asking for and for the inside of the home to be exactly like I have envisioned it. I ask for strategies in all things You are having me create, strategies of plans on how to implement these projects with such victory and success. Give charge to Your mighty angels Lord to busy themselves in making Your plans and visions for my life a reality, without any restrictions and limitations, in Jesus' name, Amen.

Do you want to continue playing yourself small? Are you ready to spend the rest of your life just trying to keep your head above the water by saying no to your next level season?

Or are you ready to believe that the King of ALL kings has put ALL the resources, tools, connections and desires for you to become who He created you to be at your disposal?

Don't you think it's time to let go of your fears and step out BIG time? What if you told our Lord of ALL lords what your heart desires and how you would use them for His glory? When you tell Him, do you trust Him to give it to you?

Proverbs 3:5-6 (NKJV)
Trust in the Lord with all your heart, and do not lean on your own understanding; In all your ways acknowledge Him, and He shall direct your paths.

You can trust Him. Tell Him the life you so desire and ask Him for the life He designed for you. Let Him know you are going to NEED Him EVERY step of the way.

Entry 28

As this writing journey comes to an end for me, the completion of this book, I am looking forward to enjoying every minute of my break time. Of course, I still have to put it together as far as the editing, re-editing, more editing, proofreading and working on my cover. I thank God for the beautiful people He has allowed me to work with on this project. During this winter season, many will be doing their best to stay warm and probably finish up their Christmas shopping or trying start their Christmas shopping. The streets will be busy with all kinds of traffic, people crowding at the malls or online rushing orders trying to get their shopping done. As for me, I am continuing to work on completing this project, another beautiful gift to myself and to the world. After all the process of getting this book edited, designed, and published, I can then just sit back and let the abundance fall into my lap. This doesn't mean I'm just going to sit here and not do anything else. I need to finish this project before I can begin on the next one. I am excited to see how this is all going to turn out. God is always doing a new thing. Every project He has me working on is never the same as the ones before it. I will continue to stay connected to Him and do my best to be in tune with Him, to hear His voice and what He is saying in this hour and every hour. The plans He has for me in 2018 will be just as exciting as this year was for me, but even more. Although 2017 is coming to an end, I have learned so much and have grown so much in my walk with Him. I will be working on researching and studying the things He is having me set up with other mighty men and women of God. We are going to shake the grounds we walk on, bringing the presence and glory of God where ever we go. I am so grateful and thankful to God for ALL He is doing. I am excited to know BIG things are coming up ahead. I may not know what it is but I do know it is coming, and I thank God that I get to be part of this BIG movement. This move of God will be taking place throughout all the face of the earth, from these little hubs no one knows about and from people who they have never heard of. Thank You God for not doing it without me. As your word says in 2 Peter 1:4 "And because of Your glory and excellence, You have given us great and precious promises. These are the promises that enable me to share Your divine nature and escape the world's corruption caused by human desires." As I wait patiently for the abundance to land in my lap, I will praise You anyhow and continue to stand on Your promises You have given us. Thank You Papa!

Below I have listed some of God's Promises to His children. There are many more but you can use these for yourself as well to help keep you going. These were given to us from our Father, Abba.

Promises

Romans 8:37-39(NLT)
No, despite all these things, overwhelming victory is ours through Christ, who loved us.

And I am convinced that nothing can ever separate us from God's love. Neither death nor life, neither angels nor demons, neither our fears for today nor our worries about tomorrow—not even the powers of hell can separate us from God's love. No power in the sky above or in the earth below—indeed, nothing in all creation will ever be able to separate us from the love of God that is revealed in Christ Jesus our Lord.

Proverbs 1:33(AMP)

"But whoever listens to me (Wisdom) will live securely and in confident trust and will be at ease, without fear or dread of evil."

Romans 10:9(AMP)

Because if you acknowledge and confess with your mouth that Jesus is Lord [recognizing His power, authority, and majesty as God], and believe in your heart that God raised Him from the dead, you will be saved.

Romans 6:23(AMP)

For the wages of sin is death, but the free gift of God [that is, His remarkable, overwhelming gift of grace to believers] is eternal life in Christ Jesus our Lord.

John 14:27(AMP)

Peace I leave with you; My [perfect] peace I give to you; not as the world gives do I give to you. Do not let your heart be troubled, nor let it be afraid. [Let My perfect peace calm you in every circumstance and give you courage and strength for every challenge.]

Isaiah 40:29-31(NLT)

He gives power to the weak and strength to the powerless. Even youths will become weak and tired, and young men will fall in exhaustion. But those who trust in the Lord will find new strength. They will soar high on wings like eagles. They will run and not grow weary. They will walk and not faint.

Matthew 11:28-30(MSG)

"Are you tired? Worn out? Burned out on religion? Come to me. Get away with me and you'll recover your life. I'll show you how to take a real rest. Walk with me and work with me—watch how I do it. Learn the unforced rhythms of grace. I won't lay anything heavy or ill-fitting on you. Keep company with me and you'll learn to live freely and lightly."

Exodus 20:12(NKJV)

"Honor your father and your mother, that your days may be long upon the land which the Lord your God is giving you."

Isaiah 54:10(NIV)

Though the mountains be shaken and the hills be removed, yet my unfailing love for you will not be shaken nor my covenant of peace be removed," says the Lord, who has compassion on you.

Isaiah 61:1(NIV)

The Spirit of the Sovereign Lord is on me, because the Lord has anointed me to proclaim good news to the poor. He has sent me to bind up the brokenhearted, to proclaim freedom for the captives and release from darkness for the prisoners,

James 1:5 (AMP)

If any of you lacks wisdom [to guide him through a decision or circumstance], he is to ask of [our benevolent] God, who gives to everyone generously and without rebuke or blame, and it will be given to him.

1 John 1:9(NIV)

If we confess our sins, he is faithful and just and will forgive us our sins and purify us from all unrighteousness.

James 4:7(AMP)

So, submit to [the authority of] God. Resist the devil [stand firm against him] and he will flee from you.

2 Chronicles 7:14(NIV)

If my people, who are called by my name, will humble themselves and pray and seek my face and turn from their wicked ways, then I will hear from heaven, and I will forgive their sin and will heal their land.

*Wealth Formula

Believe + Receive = Become

When we believe we can have wealth and then we receive wealth, we become wealthy!

Conclusion

Writing about my own personal journey regarding wealth has made it quite a learning experience for me. What I have discovered about wealth has changed my outlook on how I view the meaning of riches and its value. I am happy to say, I can move forward with a new mindset on making the right choices to be successful in all areas of my life. This new mindset entails leaving behind a poor understanding of wealth and walking into and embracing a new life of plentifulness. Now that you understand your own money story from the questions you have answered throughout this book, it's up to you on what you are going to do and what plan of action you will take to regain possession and retain your lasting wealth promised to you. I hope what I shared with you will help you on your journey to say "Goodbye to Poverty & Hello Abundance."

About the Author

Corina Mausali is an author, entrepreneur, and intercessor with a prophetic calling. She is also a deliverance minister with Set Free Outreach Ministry under the leadership of Apostle Deborah Vails. Corina has also been counseling/coaching (my invisible assets) people many years, without intentionally doing it. Her love to help people and see them get healed and restored is the reason behind her writing, as she goes through her own personal healing and deliverance in the process.

Corina is blessed to work side by side great men and women of God who are ready and willing to serve others with their God-given gifts and talents. Her obedience to write what God has placed in her heart has opened doors that no one can shut.

Connect with Corina

Facebook:

https://www.facebook.com/AuthorCorinaMausali/

Instagram:

https://www.instagram.com/corinamausali/

Twitter:

https://twitter.com/CorinaMausali

Website:

https://www.corinamausali.net/